31 LETTERS TO THE CHURCH ON PRAYING

John Piippo

Scripture taken from the Holy Bible, NEW INTERNATIONAL VERSION®. Copyright © 1973, 1978, 1984 by Biblica, Inc. All rights reserved worldwide. Used by permission. NEW INTERNATIONAL VERSION® and NIV® are registered trademarks of Biblica, Inc. Use of either trademark for the offering of goods or services requires the prior written consent of Biblica US, Inc.

ISBN: 9798357614179

BOOKS BY JOHN PIIPPO

Praying: Reflections on Forty Years of Solitary Conversations with God

Leading the Presence-Driven Church

Deconstructing Progressive Christianity

31 Letters to the Church on Discipleship

Encounters with the Holy Spirit (Co-edited with Janice Trigg)

TABLE OF CONTENTS

Introduction

I am praying for a Next Great Awakening to fall upon our churches.

Will you join me?

Dear Church,

On April 8, 1966, the cover of Time magazine had the words, in red, against a solid black background, "Is God Dead?" Five years later, on June 21, 1971, the cover of Time was red, with a drawing of the face of Jesus, and the words "The Jesus Revolution." In the spring of 1970 I was saved, caught up in this movement that was moving across our nation. So much for the death of God, in America!

I joined a campus ministry. The leaders placed a book in my hands, written by a man with an optimistic name, Bill Bright. The book was called *Revolution Now*. Pause with me here, for a moment. I was twenty-one. I was emerging from alcohol abuse and drug use. Mine was a life of poor choices and many failures. I had flunked out of college and joined the Army National Guard. My life was devoid of meaning and purpose. And then...

... it all changed. I was part of a great Revolution. I saw many of my friends give their lives to Jesus. I became a Bible reader. And I began to pray.

During that season of life, my prayers tended towards bigness. They transcended my previous secular, reductive mentality. I had come to believe in a great big God, the kind who merely speaks and launches universes into existence.

This God knew everything that can be known (omniscience), and was able to do anything that can be done (omnipotence). This was not theoretical for me. I saw God in action. I witnessed many miraculous answers to my prayers. I was discovering that, where prayer focuses, power falls. Fifty-three years later, this has not changed.

Today, in this strange world we live in, I am praying for the same God that raised Jesus from the dead to do great things in my church, and in churches across our land. I have hope and expectation, because I have seen this happen before. Out of a dark spiritual malaise (the cultural "death" of God), came the bright light of the Jesus Movement. You had to be in it to understand it.

When I pray out of my experience in that Movement, I ask God things like this.

God, raise my experience to the level of your kingdom realities.

Show me your glory.

Enable me to see the things of earth, through the lens of heaven.

Let your manifest presence fill this temple that is your Church.

Move among us in mighty ways that transcend human abilities.

Awaken your people.

Awaken me.

I also find myself praying such things, in reverse.

God, protect me from reducing you to the level of my finite experience.

Anoint me with a holy dissatisfaction in mere human accomplishments.

Transform my doubt into belief,

my fears into faith,

my pessimism into optimism,

my cynicism into hope,

my hypocrisy into authenticity,

my secularism into supernaturalism,

my low self-worth into confidence,

my doubt into assurance,

my tentativeness into boldness,

my sin into holiness,

and my laziness into discipline.

God, give us another Great Awakening, another Welsh Revival, another Azusa Street, another Jesus Movement!

I am praying for God to do something great, in our churches, across our country. How will this happen? The answer is: by prayer. In history, moves of God are always preceded, and undergirded, by praying people.

As I dream big, I remember to think small. Most, if not all, revivals in history began with a handful of people who were praying. They rarely, if ever, happened in mega-situations. Acts chapter two gives us the prototype.

They all joined together constantly in prayer,

along with the women and Mary the mother of Jesus,

and with his brothers.

How many were "they all?" If all the believers at the time were in the Upper Room, that would be a hundred and twenty. (Acts 1:15) This is not a megachurch. It is a gathering of praying people, situated in a small outpost on the edge of the Roman empire, who believe in our mega-God.

That's what this devotional book is about. That's where you come in. *I am calling you to a prayer movement.* There's no need to wait for others to join. Remember the quote from William Booth, founder of the Salvation Army? He said,

"*I'm not waiting for a move of God; I AM a move of God.*"

Consider this 31-day devotional a refueling station. You, a Move of God, are stopping to gas up. So you can stay ignited. So you would be encouraged, and on fire, in your praying life.

I present to you thirty-one entries on thirty-one aspects of a praying life. This comes out of my fifty-three years of praying experience. So much more could be said.

You and me – we form a great, praying Move of God.

That will not be contained.

John Piippo

DAY 1

Praying for a Great Awakening

Dear Church,

I want you to pray towards a move of God in your church, and in other churches.

My friend Brian Johnson is the Executive Minister of the American Baptist Churches of Michigan. He oversees 130+ churches in our state. Quite a responsibility!

Recently, Brian contacted me, along with some other leaders, and shared a vision God had given him. God told Brian to launch a prayer movement, and begin by mobilizing our churches to pray for a move of God, in every one of our ABC churches.

When I heard this, I knew two things. First, this was a from-God vision. I cannot imagine *not* desiring God to move in my church family, and beyond. Second, because of its scope and challenges, we must be led and empowered by the Holy Spirit. Divine wisdom and power that far surpasses human abilities will be needed.

Pray for a move of God in our churches.

This is the kind of thing the apostle Paul longed for. We see it in 1 Thessalonians 1:11.

> *With this in mind, we constantly pray for you,*
>
> *that our God may make you worthy of his calling,*
>
> *and that by his power he may bring to fruition your every desire for goodness*
>
> *and your every deed prompted by faith.*

Paul prays for a move of God in Colossians 1:9.

> *For this reason, since the day we heard about you,*
>
> *we have not stopped praying for you.*
>
> *We continually ask God to fill you with the knowledge of his will*
>
> *through all the wisdom and understanding that the Spirit gives...*

Paul was always praying for the churches that were under his watchful care. Let's agree that praying for God to mightily move, in other churches, is a God-thing, a good thing.

It is a big thing.

So big, that when I heard from Brian, I found myself thinking, "This is not going to happen." But, if it did happen, it would be another Awakening. It would be different. It would be grass roots, subversive as regards the kingdom of darkness, and have revolutionary impact. Again, I witnessed such things in the Jesus Revolution of the late sixties and early seventies.

A great Move of God would be powerful, and influential., compelling and attractive.

I've been in pastoral ministry since 1971. I have seen God do things that were beyond my faith, beyond my meager abilities. To be part of a group of 130+ churches, all committed to interceding for each other, gets my attention. So, little old me, who believes in great big God, has signed up.

I am recruiting you to be part of this prayer movement. I want you to join me, and Brian, our visionary leader, and get behind this.

If you are in a different denomination, or are independent, will you join us, in praying towards this vision?

Let the praying movement begin. Now.

Love,

PJ

johnpiippo@msn.com

(That's what I'm called in my church family – "Pastor John.")

EXERCISE

Pray for another Jesus Revolution.

Pray for another Great Awakening.

DAY 2

Prayer, Defined

Dear Church,

I want you to be certain of what prayer is.

Linda and I were married in August of 1973. In 2023 we will have been married fifty years!

When I met Linda, I was twenty-one years old, a college student, and a new follower of Jesus. I began attending a campus ministry. I joined one of the small groups, which met weekly. I attended large group Bible studies and worship meetings. I began forming new friendships. In that context, one of them was with Linda.

I lived with my parents, thirty miles from campus. I commuted to classes three days a week. I was freed from alcohol and drug abuse. To my parents' amazement, I was reading my Bible. To my astonishment, I became the youth leader in the Lutheran church we attended. My life was changing. I would never be the same again!

One evening, I found myself struggling with some issues in my life. I had questions I was praying about. I was in the beginning stages of learning how to listen to the voice of the Lord. I remember thinking, "Who could I call that would listen to me?" A few names of new friends came into my mind. Linda's was one of them. Intuitively, I felt she would understand what was happening in me.

I called her. She listened, while I talked. She talked, and I listened. I felt she grasping what I was trying to say. I was being helped by her responses.

Prayer is like this.

Dallas Willard defined praying as talking with God about what God and I are thinking and doing together. Martin Luther King defined praying as "conversation with God."

Prayer is a dialogical give-and-take, between me and God. Prayer is listening as well as speaking. In prayer, discernment precedes decision making.

One of the things that happens in praying is finding out what the Father wants us to do. We see this in verses like Jeremiah 42:1-2.

> [2] *Jeremiah the prophet and said to him,*
>
> *"Please hear our petition and pray to the Lord your God for this entire remnant.*
>
> *For as you now see, though we were once many, now only a few are left.*
>
> [3] *Pray that the Lord your God will tell us where we should go and what we should do."*
>
> [4] *"I have heard you," replied Jeremiah the prophet.*
>
> *"I will certainly pray to the Lord your God as you have requested;*
>
> *I will tell you everything the Lord says and will keep nothing back from you."*

Brothers and sisters, as you enter into the great conversation with God, God will tell you where you should go, and what you should do.

Love,

PJ

QUESTIONS

What is God saying to you, about you?

What does God want you to do, today?

Where is God leading you?

How are you collaborating with God?

DAY 3

Learn Prayer by Praying

Dear Pray-ers,

I want you to learn about prayer, by praying.

In 1977 I taught a course on prayer at Northern Seminary, in its Master of Divinity program. My main assignment for the students was to pray thirty minutes, every day, for twelve weeks. I knew that, in a course on prayer, students had to engage in actual praying. To *not* pray in a prayer class would be like studying swimming, while never getting in the pool.

A few students objected to this assignment. Instead of actually praying, they wanted to read books, and write papers, on prayer. How absurd! I knew my students would learn more about prayer by praying, than can be gotten from reading books (like this one!) or writing research papers. Imagine a research paper on swimming, by an author who has never entered the water.

The purpose of a swimming class is to bring us into relationship with the water. The purpose of the Bible is to bring us into relationship with God. As wonderful as God's Word is, God himself is better. When the psalmist sings "better is one day in your courts than a thousand elsewhere," it's because the presence of God is there.

It's like this. I'd rather talk with my wife Linda than read a book about her. I prefer sitting on the beaches of the Caribbean Sea, more than reading about it. I'll take eating Gino's Chicago pizza over looking at photos of it. Better to taste and see for myself, than read about how good it tasted to others.

Eugene Peterson said he wanted to do original research on praying, rather than dispense hand-outs about praying. Peterson wanted to teach from his own experience, and not live as a parasite on the first-hand spiritual lives of others.

My dear sisters and brothers, I counsel you to pray, and discover, first-hand, the possibilities and actualities available in God's presence.

Love,

PJ

ASSIGNMENT

Identify a place where you can get alone with God,

with minimal distraction,
and pray.

Begin with thirty minutes.

DAY 4

Jesus Had a Praying Life

Dear Praying Church,

Because Jesus prayed, so also are you to pray.

When I was a boy, Elvis was my hero. I wanted to be like him. I remember a day when I took an Elvis album cover into the bathroom and propped it against the mirror so I could see it. There I was, with my face in the mirror, next to the King's.

Then, I attempted to curl my lip like Elvis did when he sang. I took some hair gel and tried to recreate Elvis's hair. I began to speak like Elvis did, in that low, smoky, bluesy baritone voice. All this and more was hard work, but worth it if people would see the resemblance.

Finally, I was ready to walk into the real world. I left my house and Elvised into my friend John's backyard. I was hoping he would see that I looked like you-know-who. When he saw "Elvis," namely *moi*, John said words that shattered me. "So, you're trying to look like Elvis again."

Trying? I want to be him!

We want to be like those we worship. In many ways, we become what we worship. When I began to follow and worship Jesus, I wanted to be like him. I wrote a worship song that was recorded by some Christian artists. It was called "More Like You." I recorded it myself, and Linda and I had it played at our wedding.

To be like Jesus. To be formed into greater and greater Christlikeness. (Galatians 4:19) 1 John 3:2 says,

> *Dear friends,*
>
> *now we are children of God ,*
>
> *and what we will be has not yet been made known.*
>
> *But we know that when Christ appears,*
>
> *we shall be like him,*
>
> *for we shall see him as he is.*

What was Jesus like? Well, he prayed.

Here's my reasoning.

1. Jesus is my Great Shepherd.
2. My Great Shepherd spent much time praying.
3. Therefore, I spend much time praying.

We read these words in Luke 5:16:

> *Jesus often withdrew to lonely places and prayed.*

Jesus prayed. Often.

For decades it has been my habit, weekly, to go to a lonely place, and pray. I do this for several reasons. But mainly, I do it because this Jesus that I worship did it, and I want to be like him.

As do you.

When you look into the mirror, see the face of Jesus next to yours. He's calling you to meet with him and talk with him and listen to him, often.

Love,

PJ

CHALLENGE

Imitate Jesus's praying life.

DAY 5
God Will Tell You Something

Dear Church,

If you acquire a habitual praying life, you will often hear God saying, "I love you."

In the late 1970s I taught a Doctor of Ministry course on prayer, at Northern Seminary. One of my students was a pastor named Matt. I saw Matt as a great leader, who passionately loved Jesus. I have never forgotten the first day of that class, and what happened to Matt.

I handed out a copy of Psalm 23 to the students. I then said, "I want you to find a quiet place on the seminary campus. When you are there, meditate on Psalm 23. When God speaks to you, write it down on this paper. Do this for an hour. Then, return to class."

When the hour was over, all the students came back. Except Matt. My immediate thought was, "He doesn't like my class." What happened to him, I wondered?

The next day of class came. Matt was there. I asked about what happened in yesterday's class. Why didn't he come back? Matt said, "As I was praying, I heard God tell me that he loved me. I haven't heard God say that to me for a long time. I was so moved that I couldn't leave that place and return to the class."

Before Jesus began his earthly ministry, two things happened. He was baptized. Then, he was led by the Holy Spirit into the wilderness, to be tempted by Satan. Immediately after he was baptized, we read this.

> *Just as Jesus was coming up out of the water,*
>
> *he saw heaven being torn open*
>
> *and the Spirit descending on him like a dove.*
>
> [11] *And a voice came from heaven:*
>
> *"You are my Son, whom I love; with you I am well pleased."*

The voice of the Father could have said countless things about Jesus the Son. Like, "You will do great things." Or, "You will one day die on a cross, for the redemption of humanity." Or, "I will raise you from death to life." While all these things, and more, are awesome and true, the Father chose to say, "I love you."

In saying this, God the Father established Jesus's identity. How significant is this? We could interpret the rest of the gospels as a battle over the identity of Jesus. The conflict began, immediately, after the Father spoke, "You are my greatly loved Son, and my pleasure rests upon you."

And then...

At once the Spirit sent him out into the wilderness,

¹³ and he was in the wilderness forty days, being tempted by Satan.

Satan tempted Jesus..., to do what? To forsake his identity as Beloved Son of the Father.

Your identity has the same root as that of Jesus. You are beloved daughters and sons of the King. For God so loves you, that he sent his Son to live and die for you. It is no coincidence that these were the first words from God that I ever heard.

I was twenty-one. A campus pastor, whose name was Marshall, was talking to me and my roommate about Jesus. I wasn't listening, because I was thinking how I could argue against this pastor. I asked him a question. A hard one. I threw him an unhittable curve ball. I was hoping he would try to answer it and make a fool of himself. Instead, to my great disappointment, he responded, "I can't answer that one." Then he added, "But I do believe there is a God, and that God loves you."

That was it, for me. I was undone. My narcissistic self was struck a fatal blow. *God... loves... me.* I knew it, viscerally, existentially, ontologically. In my heart. I have never been the same. I am God's beloved.

So are you.

I find this to be a rule: I love talking with people who love me. I am in a praying, communicating, conversational love-relationship with the Lord of heaven and earth, who calls me "Beloved.".

Sisters and brothers, listen! As you live the praying life, you will hear the Father telling you, "You are my beloved child."

Love,

PJ

QUESTION

What is God saying to you, about you?

TO DO

Pray for a move of God in your church.

DAY 6

Intercession and Intersection

Dear Church,

Effective praying happens at the intersection of heaven and earth.

I live in Monroe, Michigan. Monroe is located south of Detroit, north of Toledo, on the shores of Lake Erie, and off I-75. The main north/south road that cuts through Monroe is Telegraph Road. It used to be called "bloody Telegraph," before I-75 was constructed, since it was the main, heavily congested, north-south artery connecting Detroit to Ohio.

Our church building is adjacent to Telegraph. One mile north of us is M-50, which runs from east downtown Monroe to the west.

M-50 and Telegraph Road intersect. If I were standing in the center of this intersection, which road would I be on? The answer is: I would be on both M-50 and Telegraph. At the same time. If you are a physicist, this may sound like Schrodinger's cat which, in quantum mechanics, can be both alive and dead, at the same time.

Think of an intersection. Intercessory prayer is intersectionary prayer. *We pray for others, where heaven intersects with earth.* We see this in The Lord's Prayer, when we pray, "God, let your kingdom come, let your will be done, *on earth, as it is in heaven.*"

Authentic praying happens at the intersection of earth and heaven.

We see this in 1 Timothy 2:1. *I urge, then, first of all, that petitions, prayers, intercession and thanksgiving be made for all people.* The biblical Greek word translated as 'intercession' has the sense of *to converge.* To converge, in the case of praying, is to come between God and the person we are praying for.

When I pray for others, it helps to remember that I am kneeling in the place where the resources of heaven converge with the limitations of earth. Thus, I am praying in a place of great power, love, and hope. My expectation that God is empowering my prayers makes, for me, a great praying difference.

Love,

PJ

EXERCISE

Using Colossians 1:9, fill in the blank with
someone you are interceding for.

*For this reason, since the day [I] heard about _____, [I]
have not stopped praying for _____. [I]* **continually** *ask God
to fill _____ with the knowledge of his will through all the
wisdom and understanding that the Spirit gives,*

DAY 7

Praying with Expectation

Dear Church,

Pray, with expectation that Almighty God is responding.

Recently some great Christian scholars have written books containing testimonies of miracles. J. P. Moreland has given us *A Simple Guide to Experience Miracles.* Eric Metaxas published his book *Miracles: What They Are, Why They Happen, and How They Can Change Your Life.* New Testament scholar Craig Keener has written his massive, exhaustive two-volume study *Miracles: The New Testament Evidence.* He recently published another miracles book, *Miracles Today.* And Lee Strobel has contributed *The Case for Miracles.* If you are in need of some encouragement, check these books out!

Both Keener books, and the Strobel book, contain a miracle that happened in my church family. It's about a man named Carl, who broke his ankle. This was sad for several reasons, to include that Carl was a long-distance runner who has run in the Boston Marathon more than once.

The Sunday after his accident, several in our church family prayed for Carl's ankle to be healed. To our joy, it happened! When Carl revisited the orthopedic surgeon the following week, the radiology report caused the doctor to tell Carl, "You never had a broken ankle."

I have the MRIs of Carl's foot before receiving prayer (broken ankle), and five days later (no broken ankle). You can read Carl's story in Keener, *Miracles Today* (pp. 76 ff.), and in Strobel's *Case for Miracles.* (pp. 105 ff.)

When Carl came before our church, on a Sunday morning, and gave his testimony, there was great joy and thanksgiving, given to the God who still heals! Our people were given a fresh infusion of hope, which leads to the expectation that God is moving in our midst.

A Jesus-follower in the first century would go to church gatherings expecting prayers for the sick, demons being cast out, spiritual gifts manifesting, and maybe even a dead person brought back to life. What they would see in many American churches today bears little resemblance to that.

Why would such things normally be expected? Because...

- Jesus did these kind of things
- Jesus said his followers would do these kind of things
- The Church was birthed in these things

I often tell my church family, "We are a praying church!" In a praying atmosphere we offer many prayers, and experience miracles, signs, spiritual gifts, deliverance from demonic oppression, and wonders.

My dear sisters and brothers, where prayer focuses, God's power falls. Therefore, as you pray, be expectant!

Love,

PJ

COUNSEL

Pray today with your physical eyes wide open.

Pray today with your spiritual eyes wide open.

Pray this: "God, let me see the things of earth, through the lens of heaven."

DAY 8

God Power-shares with Praying People

Dear Church,

In praying we gain access to the power of God.

I meet people, including pastors and Christian leaders, who struggle to find time to pray. My seminary teaching tells me that many North American and European pastors don't have much of a praying life. Why not? Some reasons for this are:

- Their lives have become so cluttered with many things to "do" that they have little time for just "being" with God.
- Their material possessions allow "no time to pray," and create the illusion of not needing to pray. Time for praying is in inverse proportion to the amount of stuff a person has.
- They have lost their first love. They used to get alone with God and pray, back in the day.
- They know what prayer is, but do not really believe in it. They have become practical atheists.

If prayer is what it claims to be, viz., communicating with an omniscient, omnipotent, omnibenevolent Being, then it seems someone who believed this would pray. Because praying is talking with *God*. And – (insert awe and wonder) - because God and I are co-laboring together.

To pray is to partner with God. God and I, dialoguing! Are you kidding me?! If this is real, only a fool would *not* pray. If this is *not* real, then you won't see me praying, even in a foxhole.

Dallas Willard writes: "*Prayer* is God's arrangement for a safe power sharing with us in his intention to bless the world through us." In praying I interact with God. God shares his power with me. Pause at the enormity of this. Who in their right mind would not have time for this?

Brothers and sisters, praying is a beyond-big deal. As you pray, God shares his power with you, power for effectively engaging in the redemptive mission of Jesus.

Love,

PJ

PETITION

Identify an impossible person, or situation.

Pray for God's power to fall on that person, or situation.

Pray for a prayer movement in your church.

DAY 9

Prayer Works

Dear Praying Church,

I want you to remember that your prayers work.

I pray because prayer works. If I thought prayer didn't work, I would not waste my time praying.

Praying "works." What does this mean? As I see things…,

- Prayer is powerful. Which means, it does things. (James 5:16)
- Prayer is effective. Which means, it changes things. (James 5:16)
- Praying brings me into relationship with God, experientially. I meet with God, in prayer. I experience and sense the presence of God, with me. This is important because *experience, not theory, breeds conviction.*
- I engage and co-partner with God in his redemptive mission.
- I experience God's guiding hand. I can corroborate this. I have multiple examples, written in 3500+ pages of journals, over the past forty-five years. I have read countless stories of God's guidance, from among the 4000 students and pastors I have taught.
- I have seen things happen, and change, as a result of praying. I can make a case for the causal efficacy of praying as co-laboring with God.
- I have seen how a life of praying recalibrates, daily, my heart to the heart of God.
- A life of praying has changed me. For the better, I believe. (Note: for the Christian theist "better" is understood in terms of the "best" that is Jesus.)
- I experience a life of praying that renders me less anxious, less fearful, and less lonely. This is a palpable, existential, living reality.

- I know that praying changes things and changes the one who meets with God and prays.

- While praying, I often experience brokenness within me, resulting in breakthrough outside and around me.

The 4th-century theologian John Chrysostom, in a moment of joyful realization and remembering, wrote on the efficacy of praying:

The potency of prayer hath subdued the strength of fire;

it hath bridled the rage of lions,

hushed anarchy to rest,

extinguished wars,

appeased the elements,

expelled demons,

burst the chains of death,

expanded the gates of heaven,

assuaged diseases,

repelled frauds,

rescued cities from destruction,

stayed the sun in its course,

and arrested the progress of the thunderbolt.

Prayer is an all-efficient panoply,

a treasure undiminished,

a mine which is never exhausted,

a sky unobscured by clouds,

a heaven unruffled by the storm.

It is the root, the fountain,

the mother of a thousand blessings.

(From *The Divine Liturgy of St John Chrysostom*)

James 5:16 says,

Therefore confess your sins to each other

and pray for each other so that you may be healed.

The prayer of a righteous person is powerful and effective.

Be encouraged! Your prayers work to make a holy difference.

Love,

PJ

REMEMBER

Make a list of answered prayers.

Keep adding to the list, as the Holy Spirit reminds you.

DAY 10

Healing Prayers

Dear Church,

Pray for the sick to be healed.

I was Associate Pastor at First Baptist Church of Joliet, Illinois, from 1974-1981. We had many wonderful friends there. One was a beautiful, Jesus-filled, elderly lady named Elsie. She was so kind to Linda and me. I can still hear the sound of her voice and see her smile.

Elsie had become physically frail. One day I got word that she was sick, with some kind of virus. I visited her and prayed for God to make her well. I always pray this way for sick people. So do you, right?

To be honest, I did not expect much to happen. Yet it felt good to lovingly pray for her, and she seemed to appreciate it. When I left her that day, the thought came to me that I would soon be doing her funeral. God, however, did not share my pessimism.

That evening Elsie called. Her voice was alive and vibrant. "I am feeling so much better. Thank you, John, for coming and praying for me. God has healed me!"

Really? I was happy, and stunned. We all loved Elsie so much. The illness that had a grip on her physical body was gone! To my surprise, Elsie was alive, and would be for several more years.

As significant as that experience was for Elsie, I wonder if it was not more important for me. I gained confidence in praying for people. I had a greater realization that praying is a powerful thing to do. I found that God's healing love was not corrupted by my mini-sized faith.

If your loved one was sick, you would pray for them to get better. In my church family, every Sunday, we pray for sick people to be healed. We view healing as comprehensive, and in this way Hebraic. This comprehensiveness is seen in how Eugene Peterson translates Isaiah 53:3-5, in *The Message*:

> *The fact is, it was our pains he carried —*

our disfigurements, all the things wrong with us...

He took the punishment that made us whole.

Through his bruises we get healed.

"All the things wrong with us." Physical suffering. Mental illness. Anxiety and panic. Depression. Our inadequacies and failures. Sin. The atoning sacrifice of Christ has covered all our bases. The Atonement covers sin, yes, and so much more (a lot of which is the logical outcome of our sin).

Last Sunday we prayed for sick people to be well. I talked with a number of people who told me they had pain, and after praying for them the pain was gone. People were smiling, saying that chronic pain had been taken away. They were praising God for what only he can do!

I think this is good, don't you?

I want you to keep praying for the sick, with expectation.

Love,

PJ

CHALLENGE

Identify someone who is sick.

Contact them.

Ask if you can pray for them.

Pray for them to be healed, in Jesus' name.

DAY 11

Habitual Praying Brings Transformation

Dear Believers,

People who pray experience spiritual transformation.

I have taught at Payne Theological Seminary, as an Adjunct Professor of Spiritual formation, for fifteen years. Payne is an A.M.E. seminary (African Methodist Episcopal). It is one of three black academic institutions in Wilberforce, Ohio (with Wilberforce University, and Central State University). Payne Seminary is the oldest free-standing black seminary in our nation. What a joy and privilege to teach there!

Spiritual Formation is about how God changes the human heart. The core of my class is *praying*. I know, by experience, and by Scripture, that if a student develops a habitual praying life, they will change, and never be the same again. Their spiritual lives will be green and growing.

In John chapters fourteen and fifteen Jesus shares the open secret of his success with his disciples. Which is: He is in the Father, and the Father is in him. He then invites his disciples into that Trinitarian relationship. The point of entry is given in his illustration of the Vine and the branches.

Be like a branch, says Jesus, connected to himself, the Vine. Then, he says, you will bear much fruit.

How shall we do this? Praying is a major way of abiding in Christ. As we live the abiding life, keeping in step with the Holy Spirit, God predicates, of us, the "fruit of the Spirit" (Galatians 5:22-23). Which are attributes of God himself.

I have learned that a person cannot have a consistent praying life and remain unchanged. Consider this, as an analogy. Imagine receiving a phone call from the President of the United States. I know this is never going to happen. Just, for now, use your imagination! Imagine the President of the world's most powerful nation asks if you would meet with them, for an hour, every day, to talk about how to make our nation, and the world, better. Would you clear out your schedule to do this? I know I would! The opportunity to co-labor with the world's most powerful leader would be beyond-words incredible!

Would you be affected by this? I think you would be in a state of ongoing mind-and-heart transformation. Probably, we could just look at you and see the difference. (Remember Moses when he came down from the mountain.)

Now, what if the omnipotent, omniscient, omnibenevolent, necessarily existent, all-merciful, all-gracious, all-truthful, all-compassionate Creator and sustainer of all that is, Mighty God, everlasting Father, Prince of Peace, invited you to have conversations with him, every day, about advancing his Kingdom on the earth? Would you give up chatting on social media to do this? Or your golf game, or whatever, to take time for this?

What might we conclude about someone who is too busy for this? They would be, using Jesus's metaphor, a disconnected branch, producing nothing. (John 15:5-6) Dead branches do not exhibit life-changing transformation.

Remember when Jesus told his disciples, "If you love me, you will keep my commands?" My believing brothers and sisters, *if you believe in Him, you will pray. And if praying becomes a way of life, you will walk in ongoing transformation into Christlikeness.* (Galatians 4:19)

Love,

PJ

MEDITATION

Write these words on a 3X5 card.

Carry it with you.

Read it often.

Do not be conformed to the standards of this world,

But be transformed by the renewing of your mind.

Then you will be able to discern the good and perfect will of God.

Romans 12:2

DAY 12

Hearing God

Dear Church,

To pray is not only to talk to God, but also to hear God talk to you.

One question I address in seminary classes is, "How do I hear the voice of God?" This is important, since the Lord is our Shepherd, we are his sheep, and his sheep hear his voice.

To be led by the Holy Spirit surely requires some kind of communication, from the Spirit, to us. For me, this especially happens when I am praying. My praying life forms a necessary foundation for hearing God.

The heart of true prayer is this: talking with God about what God and I are thinking and doing together. In praying, I receive divine revelation and discover God's plans and purposes for me.

I hear God, speaking to me. I situate myself in position to discern the voice of God from other voices, by doing three things.

1) First, I saturate in the Scriptures.

2) Second, I spend much time meeting with God.

3) Third, I hang around people who do 1 and 2.

Over the decades, I have learned to hear God communicating with me. For me, this has been a slow-cooker, more than a microwave.

To hear from God, don't focus on trying to hear from God. You don't have to work hard at this. Hearing doesn't come by striving.

Instead, focus on living an abiding-in-Christ life. In a life of continual abiding, which includes having a praying life (i.e., you *actually pray* for extended periods of time), my expectation is that you will begin to hear God's voice, spoken to you.

My friends, remember: *this is not about a task we have to do, but about a relationship we desire.* It's a love relationship, like daughter/ Father, or son/Father.

Desire always leads to discipline.

Love,

PJ

EQUIP

Purchase this devotional book, and use it for a year.

Hearing God Through the Year: A 365-Day Devotional,

By Dallas Willard

DAY 13

The Lord's Prayer

Dear Disciples of Christ,

I want you to pray the vast scope of The Lord's Prayer.

I was raised in a Lutheran church, in Rockford, Illinois. We were a liturgical church. In our hymnbooks there was given the order, the format, of our Sunday worship services.

There were responsive readings, and singing, in response to the pastor's singing. This included saying, every Sunday, The Apostles' Creed. The liturgical songs included Psalm 51.

"Create in me, a clean heart, O God; renew a right spirit within me.

Cast me not away from Thy presence,

Anda take not Thy Holy Spirit from me.

Restore unto me the joy of my salvation,

And renew a right spirit within me."

As I type these words, the melody of how we sang Psalm 51 is rock-solid in my soul. I have drawn upon it many times in my life.

And, we said The Lord's Prayer.

Every Sunday.

I know it by heart. So do you.

I used to think this prayer was entirely eschatological, wholly about a future kingdom, in heaven, to be experienced after I die. But as years passed, and I studied this, I came to see The Lord's Prayer as referring both to eternal life in heaven, and to my life, and our lives, on earth.

The term "kingdom," in the New Testament, refers to the rule, or reign, of God. Not only postmortem, but presently, as well. In Christ, the kingdom of heaven has invaded the kingdom of earth. New Testament scholar George Ladd says the "age to come" has penetrated this present, dark age. Thus, we followers of Jesus can expect to experience the rule and reign of God, now, wherever we are. (In theology, this is called "realized eschatology.")

Even in Michigan. Even where you live.

Even in your church family.

When I understood more about the kingdom of God, I began to pray The Lord's Prayer differently. Now, I pray like this, because I believe this is how the early Jesus-followers understood it.

God, let your kingdom come,
not only in the future,

but here,

presently,

in our experience.

God, reign over our hearts and minds,

NOW.

As we are conscious of our surroundings,

As we take our next breath,

As we walk into whatever this day has for us.

Let things be here,

in our homes,

in our church families,

in our community,

in our hearts and minds,

on this earth,

as things are in heaven.

Let us see earth, through the lens of heaven,

and respond accordingly.

Truly!

C. S. Lewis called it the "Great Invasion."

Love,

PJ

ATTENTION

Spend time looking closely at the Lord's Prayer.

What are the petitions, in this prayer?

Pray these petitions, with expectation.

Pray for heaven to invade your church family.

Pray for realities of the age to come to penetrate
and dispel this prsent darkness.

DAY 14

Habitual Praying

Dear Praying People,

Your praying times should be what you do, as usual.

This morning I received two e-mails from friends who have been desperately praying for answers from God. Today, they received those answers, and were blown away by this. One person wrote, "Why do I not expect this to happen?" Now, for the moment at least, they are motivated to pray more.

In a few minutes I will walk to the back of our property, by the river, where there is an old table, and my praying chair. I'll bring my journal, Bible, and a cup of coffee. I will meet with my God and pray.

I will pray for others. I will listen to God speak to me. And it shall be good. At this point in my life, I rarely leave these praying times without feeling encouraged and strengthened.

I pray. A lot. I do this because "Jesus went out *as usual* to the Mount of Olives, and his disciples followed him." (Luke 22:29) What Jesus did there was:

1) instruct his disciples to watch and pray.
2) pray, himself.

"As usual," Jesus went to the Mount of Olives, and prayed. "As was his habit." Praying was Jesus's customary way of doing life. Praying was a way of life for Jesus. If Jesus habitually did this, who am I, one of his followers, not to?

I heard of a sign, supposedly on the Alaskan Highway, where the road turned from pavement to dirt. It read: "Choose your rut carefully. You'll be in it for the next hundred miles."

Choose a praying life. Over time, it will become your habit, something you engage in, as usual.

Love,

PJ

COUNSEL

Identify one day, during the week, to pray for an hour.

Identify a place of least distraction, where you will do this.

Do it weekly.

DAY 15

Devotion to Praying

Dear Church,

You must devote yourself to praying.

The apostle Paul, in Colossians 4:2, instructs the Christian community in Colossae to *devote yourselves to prayer, being watchful and thankful.* The word 'devote' is intense. It has the following meanings.

To adhere to someone or something.

To be steadfastly attentive.

To persevere and not to faint.

To be devoted to prayer means...

... gluing yourself to the act of praying

... making a praying life your priority

... never giving in to prayerlessness, even, and especially, when life is hard.

Linda and I have a framed saying on display in our home. It reads, "You have my whole heart, for my whole life." I see it every day, multiple times. I love those words! I know about this thing called devotion. I am devoted to my wife Linda. I am spiritually glued to her, in a bond of covenant love. I love being with her.

As a young man I was devoted to learning to play guitar. No one had to tell me that I had to practice. I wanted, so badly, to play well!

When a person is devoted to something, you won't be able to separate them from the object of their devotion.

Apply this to praying.

Be devoted to prayer.

Persevere, and do not faint.

Give unremittingly to meeting with God and praying.

This is core Christian behavior. We see it in the early, prototypical church.

They devoted themselves to the apostles' teaching and to fellowship, to the breaking of bread and to prayer.

(Acts 2:42)

I want you, and your church, to emulate this.

Love,

PJ

DEVOTION

Devote yourself to praying for a Move of God
in your church, and beyond.

Be like William Booth, who viewed himself as a Move of God.

DAY 16

Jesus-lovers Pray

Dear Church,

Praying is not something you have to do. But if you love him, you will pray.

Linda and I have two grandchildren. We love them! Our love does not come out of a sense of duty. I could not imagine saying to them, as they get older, "I love you, because I am supposed to love you."

We agree that, yes, we have a God-given duty to cherish our grandchildren. But the love of God transcends a sense of duty.

This is all about intimate relationship.

Praying is a way of being-in-relationship-with God. It is not a religious duty that one *has* to do. Praying has its roots in the soil of God's love. As Jesus said, "If you love me, keep my commands." (John 14:15) One of which is to watch, and pray.

For eighteen years I was a professor of logic at our local community college. Jesus employed logic and reason. Those who love Jesus keep his commands, one of which is to pray. Logically, it looks like this.

1. If I love Jesus, I will pray.
2. I love Jesus.
3. Therefore, I pray.

Or,

4. If I love Jesus, then I will pray.
5. I don't pray.
6. Therefore, I don't love Jesus.

This is not rocket science. We do what we love. Love (desire) without discipline is an illusion. Intentions minus actions equal nothing. I communicate with Linda, not because I "have to," but because I love her. I desire to be in relationship with her. To only talk and listen to her out of duty would signify a strange, unsatisfying, colorless marriage.

Prayer is a relationship, not a transaction. When praying erodes from "I want to" into "I have to," joy diminishes. Mere dutiful praying has little connection to life.

Praying is not something we have to do. To pray is to be in relationship with God. When you are in a loving relationship with someone, you communicate.

My dear brothers and sisters: *If you love Him, you will pray.*

Love,

PJ

EXAMEN

Search your heart.

Don't lose sight of your first love.

DAY 17

Prayer and Purpose

Dear Church,

People who pray find their work purposeful.

I have a friend who loves to work in his large vegetable and flower garden. He talks about needing "garden time." I say to him, "That's your therapy."

Working and laboring for a purpose brings satisfaction. (For an example of working for no purpose, read atheist Albert Camus's *The Myth of Sisyphus*.)

In praying, God gives me work orders. In the praying room with God, I receive his kingdom plans and purposes. Life-purpose grows as I pray in the garden of God's presence.

Presence is prior to purpose. Purpose comes out of prayerful presence. In praying, I hear the call of God to "Go," or "Do." Famously, my *doing* emerges out of my *being*. My activity emerges from my praying times with God. Allow me to illustrate.

Linda and I enjoy food shopping together. I like collaborating with her about meal planning. She mostly has a better sense about this than I do. Klondike bars only go so far when it comes to nutrition.

Sometimes, I food shop without Linda. She appreciates this. I embark carrying a list of items we need, authored mostly by her. But, alas, I have sometimes gone into the food wilderness without a list. At this point, anything is possible.

For example, I went to the store to pick up items I thought we needed. I had not consulted Linda. Like a sojourner in a strange land, I was in the store, listless.

I came to the aisle containing spaghetti sauces. I marveled at the wide variety of choices shelved before me. We need, I thought, spaghetti sauce.

When I arrived home with a few bags of groceries, I proudly showed them to my wife. "Look at this," I said, as I pulled out a jar of spaghetti sauce. I handed it to Linda. She took it, walked to the cupboard, and placed it next to six jars of the same sauce.

I cannot remember her response. I am certain it was gentle, as she found the strength to say, "John, no more spaghetti sauce, please."

Lesson (hopefully) learned (again)!

Henri Nouwen was once asked, "Why did Jesus pray?" Nouwen responded, "To find out what the Father wanted him to do."

My friends, refuse to go forth into the arena of ministry without first consulting your heavenly Father.

Love,

PJ

PURPOSE

Discern what the Father is doing.

Join him there.

Ponder the implications of John 5:19-20.

DAY 18

Small Callings

Dear Church,

As you pray God will call you to do small things.

In the Spring of 1970, I turned my life over to the lordship of Jesus. Within a month, God did one of the greatest things that has ever happened in my life.

It happened on a Sunday. I was living with my parents. Church was over, and we were home. My mother had made one of her delicious, home-made-from-scratch, dinners. Afterwards, as was my custom, I went to our family room, slid into the large La-Z-Boy, and watched football, while falling in and out of sleep.

From this position, God spoke to me. He did not say, "John, gird up your loins. I am sending you to preach before tens of thousands." Instead, he said, "Go back into the kitchen and do the dishes."

I am embarrassed to say that I rarely did the dishes, while living in my parents' house. My mother always did them. I rarely cleaned up after myself. My mother always made my bed. She washed my clothes. And she made sure the freezer always contained ice cream. I was the recipient of my mother's servanthood.

On that Sunday, this all changed.

In my praying times I had been learning to discern the voice of God from other voices. I got out of the La-Z-Boy, went into the kitchen, and announced to my mother, "I am going to do the dishes."

"No, no, Johnny," she protested. "I'll do the dishes. You go watch football." She would never have added, as I might have, "Wake up, get your posterior out of that chair, and do something to help, for heaven's sake!"

My mom got a lot of her self-worth from serving and cleaning and washing and vacuuming and making beds and keeping the house beautiful. I did not want to take that away from her. But God was speaking to me. It was time to step up my game.

My mother ended up watching, out of the corner of her eye,

perhaps in awe and unbelief, as I washed the dishes. That was the day her son became a servant.

When you pray, the Holy Spirit will often prompt you to do something. God may instruct you to call someone, or visit a friend, or go someplace, or help a needy person, or serve in your church. The Holy Spirit may lift you out of your somnambulant sluggishness, walk you into the kitchen, and position you before the dirty dishes in the sink.

As you pray, God will speak to you. He will call you to acts of service and ministry. You must remember that, from God's POV, there's no such thing as a small call. Those who begin with the dishes may inherit the nations. Remember what Jesus once said, in the parable of the bags of gold.

'Well done, good and faithful servant!

You have been faithful with a few things;

I will put you in charge of many things.

Come and share your master's happiness!'

Matthew 25:23

I am a dishwasher in my house. When doing dishes, I often remember The Small Call that was gifted to me.

As you pray, listen for the voice of God. He will guide your path. What seems an insignificant thing, or a tiny calling, is never, in God's mind, small or insignificant.

Love,

PJ

ATTEND

Take care of the small things God has called you to.

DAY 19
Answering Prayer

Dear Praying Church,

You are the answer to someone else's prayer.

Often, while praying, my mind wanders to a person. I feel God placing this person on my heart, as a burden. This can mean that I am the one God is going to use, as God's answer to that person's prayer.

Here's a recent example. During my praying time, I felt led to pray for a man. Let's call him "X." While praying, I did not know that, in that very moment, X left his workspace, went to a place where he could be alone, and was praying.

X had learned that his spouse was having a sexual affair with another man. She filed for divorce. X wanted to secure help for their marriage. She refused.

That morning X received a phone call from his father. "Your mother has cancer. She's not expected to live much longer." X felt his knees buckle, his breathing difficult, the weight too much to bear. X had to get alone with the only One who could make a way where there seemed to be no way. X prayed, "God, help me... Help us!"

Meanwhile I was alone, in my backyard by the river, sitting in my prayer chair, as X was appealing to God. As I prayed the thought came to me, "Call X now." I did. I assumed this thought was coming from God to me.

I have learned, over decades of praying, listening, and risking, that God often comes as an interruption, in my "wandering mind." What could I lose from calling X to check in? This was a no-fail spiritual situation.

I called X. He answered, "I can't believe you called me. I couldn't focus on my job. I had to get alone with God. I was just asking God to send help. And then you called!"

We agreed this was no coincidence. It was the orchestrating work of the Holy Spirit. In that moment I was God's answer for X. This was God saying, "I hear X's cry. I am going to answer X's prayer by placing the thought of X in John's mind."

Here is an example from Acts chapter 9. We see the apostle Paul, who has been struck with blindness. He hasn't eaten or drank anything for three days. He is praying. In a vision, Paul sees help coming. Who might that be?

> [10] *In Damascus there was a disciple named Ananias.*
> *The Lord called to him in a vision, "Ananias!"*
> *"Yes, Lord," he answered.*
> [11] *The Lord told him, "Go to the house of Judas on Straight Street*
> *and ask for a man from Tarsus named Saul,*
> *for he is praying.*
> [12] *In a vision he has seen a man named Ananias come*
> *and place his hands on him to restore his sight."*

Ananias was the answer to Paul's prayer.

When you pray, listen for the voice of God. When an interruptive thought comes, check it out. You will begin to discover that such things can be from God.

This increases your faith and expectation.

You are being used by God to help others in their prayer-cries for mercy and rescue.

My dear friends, life in Christ is a series of interruptions. The interruptions become your life.

Love,

PJ

RESPOND

Contact that person whom God has laid on your heart.

DAY 20
Focused Praying

Dear Church,

To listen to God in prayer requires focus.

In what is arguably the most influential sermon ever given, Jesus, in Matthew 5:8, says:

> *Blessed are the pure in heart,*
>
> *For they will see God.*

What is purity of heart? The Danish philosopher Soren Kierkegaard said, "Purity of heart is to will one thing." With this in mind, here is my translation of Matthew 5:8.

> *Blessed are the mono-taskers,*
>
> *For they will see God.*

Real praying requires laying your multi-tasker down. We see this in the garden, on the week of Jesus's suffering and death. Jesus asks his disciples to watch and pray.

Watch. Pray.

Be alert.

Focus.

Real prayer mono-tasks the God-relationship. It has no agenda other than to be with our Lord.

When I go to a place of least distraction to pray, I carry with me my journal, my Bible, and a devotional book. (For example, for years I used *A Guide to Prayer for Ministers and Other Servants.*) I lay my cell phone down. If Linda calls, I will answer.

In that quiet place, I watch. I clear away mental clutter (see 1 Peter 5:7). As I do this, spiritual alertness increases.

Effective praying requires giving Jesus my undivided attention. As this happens, hearing His voice happens.

I want you to learn the beauty of mono-tasked praying.

Love,

PJ

DECLUTTER
Clear away spiritual hindrances in your heart.

DAY 21
The Wandering Mind

Dear Church,

When your mind wanders while praying, it wanders to a burden.

The first seminary class I ever taught was after I graduated from Northern Baptist Theological Seminary. It was the spring of 1977, and my theology professor, Tom Finger, asked me: "What class do you think we need in our theology department?"

"We need a class on prayer," I responded. Tom said: "I want you to teach it."

I did.

Since then, I have taught on prayer in several seminaries, pastors' retreats, and seminars and church conferences, in the U.S. and around the world. My estimate is that between four and five thousand pastors and Christian leaders have taken my courses on praying and spiritual formation.

When I teach, I assign my students to pray. I ask them to keep a spiritual journal. "When God speaks to you," I instruct, "write it down in your journal." A common concern is this. Students will write me, asking, "I am taking time to pray. But sometimes my mind wanders so much, that I cannot focus on praying. What can be done about this?" Here is what I tell them.

When your mind wanders while you are praying, it always wanders to something like a burden. Identify the burden. Then, employ 1 Peter 5:7, which counsels, "Cast your burdens on him, for He cares for you."

Note this: the less you spend time praying, the more will burdens accumulate, unaddressed, in your heart. A burden-free heart is in direct proportion to your praying life.

One more thing. When your mind wanders to a burden, about a person or a situation, this can be the Holy Spirit leading you to pray towards that event, and for that person.

My dear friends, do not focus on your burdens, but on making times to get in God's presence and pray, and experience an unburdened life.

Love,

PJ

JOURNAL

Write down where your mind wanders to.

DAY 22
Prayer and Purification

Dear Church,

Spiritual and emotional detoxifying happens when you pray.

I have, on my computer laptop, antivirus software. This program scans my laptop and sends me reports of threats that have been removed, and viruses it has exorcised. My laptop gets detoxified.

Praying does this for me. Praying de-pollutes me. Praying unburdens me.

Sometimes, when I get alone to pray, I have a fear of the unknown, or am anxious about a hard situation. I might think of a person who has misunderstood me, or a situation I am facing that seems to have no solution. Philippians 4:6 counsels us to be anxious for nothing. Sometimes, I am anxious about nothing I can identify.

Anxiety and worry are toxic viruses that threaten our spiritual and emotional well-being. Praying detoxifies the human heart.

I have had a praying life for five decades. I have seen that a praying life brings detoxification and purification. If I did not have a habitual, disciplined praying life, deadly pollutants would take up residence in my spiritual and emotional being. 1 Peter 5:7 says,

Cast your burdens on him,

For he cares for you.

My brothers and sisters, acquire a disciplined praying life. One outcome will be this. You will, more and more, experience the Holy Spirit's antiviral, protective, cleansing agency.

Blessings,

PJ

UNBURDEN

Learn, by practicing, how to cast your burdens on Jesus.

Begin by identifying a burden and writing it in your journal.

Cast the burden onto the pages of your journal.

DAY 23
Prayer and Anxiety

Dear Praying Church,

A praying life is an anxiety-buster.

Many people, to include Christians, struggle with anxiety. This includes me. I have had my anxious moments.

Jesus addresses anxiety in John 14:1, as he counsels his disciples, "Do not let your hearts be troubled." Jesus said this, knowing his disciples' hearts *were* troubled.

The biblical Greek word for 'troubled' can be translated as 'agitated.' Like the agitator of a washing machine goes back and forth, so the human heart can go back and forth, up and down. Agitation, troubledness, anxiety – they can all refer to a negative condition of the heart.

Anxiety produces nothing that is good. Thus, in Philippians 4:6, Paul counsels Jesus-followers to "be anxious about nothing." The biblical Greek word for 'anxious' is often used in contexts where persecution is happening. For example, in Matthew 10:19, Jesus counsels his disciples: "When they arrest you, do not be *anxious* about what to say or how to say it." Here the word 'anxious' is related to 'worry.'

When Paul counsels the Philippians to not worry, it's not like he's sitting on the beach, savoring a latte. He's in prison! The admonition to not worry comes in an atmosphere of fear and persecution. The Philippian Jesus-followers were suffering under opposition from their pagan neighbors, like Paul and Silas suffered when among them (Acts 16:19-24; Phil 1:28-30).

I know what anxiety is. I have experienced it in troubling times. How realistic is it to be told "Be anxious for nothing" when you are facing hard circumstances?

Paul's answer, emerging out of his experience, is found in his rich, ongoing prayer life. He writes:

Do not be anxious about anything,
but in every situation,

by prayer and petition,

present your requests to God.

Philippians 4:6-7

Henri Nouwen had a proof that prayer works. (See Nouwen, *Gracias! A Latin American Journal.*) Nouwen said when he didn't pray, he was more easily filled with fear, worry, agitation, troubledness, and anxiety. But, as he lived a praying life, God diminished these things.

A consistent praying life works to stop the inner agitator. I experience God as a great Counselor and Caregiver who casts out my fears. It is in praying that I come to know, by experience, that I have a Father God who loves me, and whom I trust.

Worry and anxiety cannot co-exist with trust. Trust is established in the heart of a person who prays. In praying, we place our burdens on Jesus, for he cares for us. (1 Peter 5:7)

My dear brothers and sisters, bring your anxieties and fears to the Lord, in prayer, and discover that he cares for you.

Love,

PJ

TODAY

Let this day be a day of trusting the Lord.

Repeat, "I trust You, Lord."

DAY 24

Prayer and Unbusyness

Dear Church,

I want you to slow down and be unbusy before God.

In 1981 God called me to a deeper praying life. I needed it so badly! I was doing, doing, doing, and the inner fire was leaving, leaving, leaving. God told me to take Tuesday afternoons, get unbusy, and pray. I needed to tend the fire within.

This was a new beginning for me, a time when my *doing* began to emerge from my *being in God*. This was important, since in the spiritual life *being precedes doing.*

That first Tuesday afternoon was spent sitting on a rusty tractor, in a field, in a forest preserve north of Lansing, Michigan. I remember *being* there, trying to pray, while my mind kept asking, "Just what the heck am I *doing* here, anyway? What am I *accomplishing*?"

The answer seemed to be: "nothing." I wasn't xeroxing. I wasn't at some planning meeting. I was producing nothing. No empirical "product" was coming from sitting on this old tractor. And yet...

...That was one of the most important days of my life. I was getting reattached to Jesus, the Vine!

Prayer is wasting time with God. The world says, "If you are not making good use of your time, you are useless." Jesus says: "Come spend some useless time with me.""

Henri Nouwen writes: "If we think about prayer in terms of its usefulness to us—what prayer will do for us, what spiritual benefits we will gain, what insights we will gain, what divine presence we may feel—God cannot easily speak to us. But if we can detach ourselves from the idea of the usefulness of prayer and the results of prayer, we become free to "waste" a precious hour with God in prayer. Gradually, we may find, our "useless" time will transform us, and everything around us will be different." (Nouwen, *Spiritual Formation: Following the Movements of the Spirit*)

The world measures us by how much we do, how much we accomplish. We impress others by how busy we are, by datebooks filled with engagements, deadlines to be met, and meetings to attend. Jesus, on the other hand, calls us to do nothing, accomplish nothing, until we first spend much time with him. "Be like a tree branch," counsels Jesus, "that stays attached to the trunk of the tree." Then, your life will bear much fruit.

I confess to having led church meetings where we decide on what we are going to do, and then baptize our decisions with prayers. The opposite, counter-intuitive way of Jesus is to first spend much time praying and, in that God-seeking environment, discern what the Lord would have us do.

In a sense, prayer is being unbusy with God, instead of being busy with other things. Prayer is primarily doing nothing useful or productive in the presence of God. If anything important or fruitful happens through prayer, then we work hard, and behold how God achieves the result.

Love,

PJ

REFUSE

Refuse to identify your worth by...

...your accomplishments, by...

...your datebook, by...

...your checkbook, by...

...your material possessions, by...

...your appearance, by...

...your performance, by...

...what others think of you.

DAY 25

Purging Prayers

Dear Church,

As you pray, God will purge you of unrighteous anger.

One result of an ongoing praying life is that God removes unrighteous anger from my heart. God takes the chip off my shoulder. He softens the edge. He forms his heart of compassion, in me, for my enemies.

Remember the prayer of Jesus, when on the cross? "Father, forgive these people who are torturing me, for they have no idea of what they are doing."

In praying, God frees me from the prison cell of hatred, and releases me to love in ways I have never done before. For me this is not a theory, but an existential reality.

My wife Linda has seen the results. Because I have a praying life, I am a better husband, father, friend, and pastor. As Christ is more deeply formed in me, I get changed.

Most of this happens as I am praying.

In praying, I am clay on a potter's wheel. I am not the agent of my own transformation, God is. Many times, I can *feel* Him shaping me.

This is praying as an act of resistance to the common, unholy structures of the world, which demand conformation to their will. To pray is to protest against the hate-filled standards of our culture. In praying we are transformed from reactionaries to revolutionaries.

Henri Nouwen says that praying is an act of protest against a world of manipulation, competition, rivalry, suspicion, defensiveness, anger, hostility, mutual aggression, destruction, and war. People who have praying lives are witnesses to the all-embracing, all-healing power of God's love. (See Nouwen, *The Road to Peace.*)

As praying becomes your *modus operandi,* God will save you from yourself.

Love,

PJ

UNDERSTAND

Anger is the emotion we feel

when one of our expectations has not been met.

Are your expectations godly?

In your anger, do not sin.

DAY 26

Preconditions for Effective Praying

Dear Saints,

Righteousness is a precondition for effective praying.

Imagine this (which is *not* an example from my family).
You have an adoscent child who has chosen to reject your counsel. You see them making choices that are destructive. Recently, they caused an accident that damaged your car, and hurt another person. They still live in your home. You decide to set some boundaries. You are not to enable their bad behavior.

Your son is not in a right relationship with you. One day he petitions you, saying,"I want the car keys. I need to go do something." Do you comply? "Not," you respond, "until we have a talk and get on the same page." The petition of an unrighteous son is powerless and ineffective.

It is the same with prayer. James 5:16 tells us this:

> *The prayer of a righteous person*
> *Is powerful and effective.*

"Righteousness" means being in right relationship with God. A righteous person is on the same moral and spiritual page as God is. Conversely,

> The prayer of an unrighteous person
> is powerless and ineffective.

"Effective."

The prayers of a person who is in right relationship with God "effect" things. This is about causality. Their prayers do things.

Brothers and sisters, righteous and holy living is a precondition for effective, powerful praying.

Love,

PJ

FOCUS

Righteousness

Holiness

Purity

Walk in step with the Spirit

*If we confess our sins, God is faithful and just and
will purify us from all unrighteousness.*
(1 John 1:9)

DAY 27

Pray for Your Enemies

Dear Church,

Pray for your enemies.

A pastor is a shepherd of people who are, metaphorically, his flock. What a privilege this is! I thank God, often, for calling Linda and me to be pastors.

But sometimes, the sheep bite. As a pastor, I have suffered my share of wounds. I've been doing the pastor thing since 1971, and I've got bite marks on my soul. Here's one story of a sheep who assaulted me.

I was in my fourth year at a church in the Chicago area. I was teaching a series, on Sunday evenings, on the book of Revelation. Which is a hermeneutical adventure, right? A number of points are up for disagreement.

At one point we were looking at the Second Coming of Christ. When will this happen? I was using Jack Hayford's *Spirit-Filled Life Bible*. Jack did the footnotes. In a footnote relevant to the question, he presented nine possible theological views of when the Second Coming might happen. I showed these to the class. I remember telling them that we need to be humble about this subject, because good Christians had differing views.

Little did I know that, as I talked about the nine possibilities, a man in the class was getting angrier and angrier. He believed there was only one view of the Second Coming, and it was his.

I have not forgotten what happened as the class ended. He was a big man, over six feet tall. He was much older than I. He approached me, bent down to my eye level. The veins in his neck were bulging. His face was red. His teeth were white. His tonsils, beet red.

He yelled at me.

I was, he said, wrong, a heretic, and a false teacher. At one point I thought he was going to hit me.

I was shaken.

As I drove home with Linda, I found myself hating him. I wanted to get even with him. Vengeance was mine, sayeth myself.

I could not pray without, in my mind, hurting him, perhaps launching a nuclear weapon, aimed at his head?

I know these thoughts are not Jesus-thoughts. Yet, I viewed him as an enemy that threatened me. He was a persecutor, of me. I could not, I chose not to, pray for him.

Making things harder, I was a lover of Jesus. I knew what Jesus said in Luke 6:28 - *Bless those who curse you, pray for those who mistreat you.* So God, how can I do this thing that you command me to do?

"Pray for your enemies," my Lord Jesus says. Well, that's easy for him to say, because he is Jesus. But not really, right? Jesus did it in the moment when hanging on that cross, as hatred assaulted him. In his darkest time, he prayed, "Forgive these people, for they don't know what they are doing."

How can I do Mark 11:25?

> *And when you stand praying,*
>
> *if you hold anything against anyone, forgive them,*
>
> *so that your Father in heaven may forgive you your sins."*

Or Mark 5:44?

> *But I tell you, love your enemies*
>
> *and pray for those who persecute you,*

And what does Psalm 23 mean when it says,

> *"You prepare a table before me in the presence of my enemies.*
> *You anoint my head with oil.*
> *My cup overflows."*

Once, while engaging with the 23rd Psalm, one of my seminary students received a God-insight I had never thought of before. God told him that, not only is the "prepared table" visible to one's enemies, but so is being anointed with oil and the overflowing cup. This cup, said my student, overflows onto our enemies!

That sounded like a God-thought to me. I related it to my cry for a greater love, in me. Anyone, it says in the Bible, can love people who love them back. That's easy. The real test is to love those who assault and endanger me.

Dear Beloved of God, there is a praying life that is deeper and wider and higher and longer, which includes praying for your enemies. I invite you to pray this with me: "God, let your love so shape and fill my heart that it overflows even onto my enemies."

Pray for release. Pray for the freedom to love others as Christ loves them.

Pray to receive this love for your own self.

Love...,

PJ

ASSIGNMENT

Pray for a love that, like the love of God, is higher, wider, deeper, and longer than any earthly love you have experienced.

DAY 28

Praying and Giving Thanks

Dear Church,

Let thanksgiving fill your hearts as you pray.

I make lists of things I am thankful for. I enshrine these in my spiritual journal. I write them on 3X5 cards, and carry them with me. I keep the list before me, re-reading and re-pondering it throughout the day. The result is, I often experience a heart that overflows with gratitude towards God. This is a good spiritual place for me to be. It also affects my times of praying.

The apostle Paul says our prayers should be accompanied "with thanksgiving." In Philippians 4:6 we read,

Do not be anxious about anything,

but in every situation,

by prayer and petition,

with thanksgiving,

present your requests to God.

New Testament scholar Ben Witherington has written that Paul believes there is much to be said for praying in the right spirit or frame of mind. This is significant for the Roman Philippians, since pagan prayers did not include thanksgiving. Roman prayers were often fearful, bargaining prayers, not based on a relationship with some god.

Witherington adds: "Prayer with the attitude of thanksgiving is a stress-buster." John Wesley said that thanksgiving is the surest evidence of a soul free from anxiety.

Paul's antidote for worry and anxiety is *praying, with thanksgiving.*

Love,

PJ

(There can be clinical, neurophysical conditions that cause anxiety and fear. The antidote for such conditions may be

medications. If you have severe anxiety I recommend two things:
 1) Praying, and having people pray for you.
2) Seeing a physician who is skilled in treating you physically.

Combine spiritual intervention with medical intervention.)

JOURNAL

Write a list, in your journal, of things you are thankful for.

DAY 29

When It's Hard to Pray

Dear Church,

Sometimes it is hard to pray.

In 1985 Linda was pregnant, expecting twins. We were thrilled about this! I remember working together to prepare a room for them. I subscribed to a magazine called "Twins." I celebrated this awaited event!

Soon, two baby boys would be in our life. Until…

I remember the routine doctor visit. The stethoscope. The doppler. The doctor. The look on his face. He told us to go to Sparrow Hospital, immediately.

One of our little boys was dead. The other was on the edge of life and death. An emergency C-section brought them both into the bright, antiseptic room. I will never forget the weight of my son David, as I held him. The other, Joshua, was being attended to.

On that day Linda and I entered the valley of the shadow of death. And it was hard to pray. In my praying time the day before, I read these words.

> *Those who sow with tears*
> *will reap with songs of joy.*
>
> *⁶ Those who go out weeping,*
> *carrying seed to sow,*
> *will return with songs of joy,*
> *carrying sheaves with them.*

Psalm 126:5-6

Sometimes, when I pray, my mind wanders. After the loss of David, and the fight for Joshua's life, "wanders" was not the word to describe my experience. In our grieving it felt like being in a black hole that devours whatever light there is.

Through it all, we are certain God understood our struggle. I remember us standing, in the hospital, looking through the window and seeing little Joshua, when one of us said, "This is hard. But imagine how hard it would be if we did not have God."

Prayers offered in the dark valley feel extraordinary compared to praying in the ordinary. During such times, do not feel less than loved and less understood by God.

In times when you are weak, and it is hard to find words, remember that Jesus himself was a man of sorrows, acquainted with grief.

Love,

PJ

P.S Our Joshua made it, and today lives a flourishing life.

REMEMBER

Express your grief to God.

Remember that Jesus was a man of sorrows, acquainted with grief. (Isaiah 53:3)

Remember that we do not have, in Jesus, a high priest who is unable to sympathize with our weaknesses. (Hebrews 4:15)

DAY 30

A Prayer Movement

Dear Church,

I want you to launch a prayer movement that will influence many.

I began this book by issuing a call to prayer, for a move of God in our churches. You do know, don't you, that every awakening, every revival, began with, and was fueled by, praying people. Here's one example.

I am especially moved by the story of a man who called his business colleagues to pray. It was 1857, in Boston. A businessman named Jeremiah Lanphier was led by God to host weekly noon prayer meetings for workers in Boston's business district. A local church gave Lanphier permission to use their facility. The format was simple. No preaching, just praying, worship, and prayer requests.

The first gathering was on September 23, 1857. Six people showed up. Next week, there were twenty. The week after, almost forty. By the end of October there were one hundred. Word of these meetings spread. Another church was needed to host what came to be known as the Fulton Street Prayer Meetings.

On March 28, 1858, 6100 people gathered, at various locations in Boston, to pray and worship. At one place there was 600, at another 1200. This was a move of God that spread to many cities across our land.

Could this happen again? I believe it not only can, but it must. We need a mighty, earth-shattering, paradigm-shifting move of God in our churches. It is time to be part of something great, for the cause of Christ. This means me. This means you.

J. P. Moreland, in his book on miracles, wrote this.

> "I would rather have the Lord take me home
> than risk failing to finish well,
>
> hurting those who look up to me, or losing my integrity."

(Moreland, *A Simple Guide to Experience Miracles*, p. 23)

Upon reading this, I reached for a 3X5 card, and wrote down the quote. I placed it in my pocket. I carried it with me for a few weeks, reading it often.

This quote became a prayer. I prayed the words to God, asking him to protect and guide me so I might finish my life well.

I think of what Jesus said, in Luke 12, about watchfulness and readiness.

"Be dressed ready for service and keep your lamps burning…

It will be good for those servants whose master
finds them watching when he comes.

t will be good for those servants whose master finds them ready,

even if he comes in the middle of the night…

You also must be ready,

because the Son of Man will come at an hour
when you do not expect him."

DAY 31

Prayer Journaling

I've been keeping a spiritual journal for fifty-three years. I have read and responded to over 3000 spiritual journals that pastors and Christian leaders have sent me, as part of seminary classes, retreats, and conferences I have taught. Here are my thoughts on keeping a spiritual journal.

A spiritual journal is a record of the voice and activity of God, to you. When God speaks to you, write it down. To do that is to keep a prayer journal.

People write differently. Some include lots of detail, such as the place where they are praying, prayer concerns, and biblical exegesis. But the core of the journal is: God's words, spoken to you. When I read the journals of others, that's what I am looking for. What is God saying to you? What is God doing with you?

When your mind wanders, I suggest writing where it wanders to. The mind does not wander arbitrarily, but always to something like a burden. The wandering mind is a barometer of your spiritual condition. Then, following 1 Peter 5:7, "cast your burdens on God, for he cares for you."

I find it helpful to get the burdens on paper. To see them on paper makes it feel like they are not inside me any longer. Now, it's at a distance from me. De-burdening is an important part of entering into God's presence more fully. We have a greater focus on God because we are not so distracted by our burdens.

If keeping a spiritual journal is writing down what God says to me, how can I know it's really the voice of God? I have found that one better hears God's voice when they:

1) Saturate themselves with Scripture.
2) Spend MUCH time alone in God's presence.
3) Hang around people who do 1 and 2.

There are some good books about this, such as Dallas Willard's

Hearing God: Developing a Conversational Relationship with God.

Because the spiritual journal is a record of God's voice to you, it is fruitful to occasionally re-read and re-meditate on your journal. A number of the things God tells you will become thematic in your life. It is important to remember them.

"Remembering" is huge in a person's spiritual life. When we have a written record of God's words for us, it can be easier to recall them as we re-ponder them anew. The maxim here is: "I will not forget God's words to me."

A spiritual journal, because it is a record of God's voice to you, is about you. Not others. Yes, I sometimes write about others in my journal. For example, I pray for others. Or, If I'm upset with someone, I use letters such as 'X' to refer to those persons. I don't want my journal to be found or read by someone with whom I'm angry. When I write down such things before God I'm primarily asking God to help, not 'X,' but me, and with any anger inside me.

What can you expect God to say to you? My experience tells me that God will say things like:

his love for you,

things he wants to heal inside you,

things you need to repent of in your life,

that he forgives you,

things about his essence (the glory of who he is),

giving you deeper insights on Scripture, giving direction, and so on.

And, God imparts his heart to you. When this happens to me I write down things like grace, mercy, peace, joy, love, hope, and power.

I don't believe journaling is for everybody. But remembering is. So is entering deeply into God's presence and hearing his voice.

***

For more on prayer and hearing God, see my book *Praying: Reflections on 40 Years of Solitary Conversations with God.*

DAY 32

One Day Jesus Was Praying

Dear Church,

I am reading, slowly, through the Gospel of Luke. This morning I began in Luke 11:1:

> *One day Jesus was praying in a certain place.*

I can't get past this verse. It's enough for me.

The verse does not say:

One day Jesus thought about praying.

It doesn't read:

One day Jesus desired to pray, but didn't have time for it.

It's not:

One day Jesus read a book about praying.

Nor does it say...

One day Jesus said, "I believe in the power of prayer."

It does say:

> *One day Jesus was praying.*
>
> *One day Jesus was actually doing it.*
>
> *One day Jesus was engaged in praying.*
>
> *One day Jesus, my Lord,*
> *my exemplar,*
> *my mentor,*
> *was spending considerable time talking with God.*

One of his followers saw him doing this. This follower was so impressed that he wanted to do what Jesus was doing. Which was:

communicating with the Maker of Heaven and Earth.

When Jesus finished dialoguing with God, the follower who desired to do the same said to Jesus, "Mentor, teach us to do what you just did."

Thank you, my praying friends for reading my thoughts on a praying life.

Please know this - the Holy Spirit is our present Teacher on prayer.

I bless you with a deep, powerful praying life that, more and more, emulates that of our Lord Jesus!

John Piippo

johnpiippo@msn.com

johnpiippo.com

Made in United States
Troutdale, OR
08/14/2024

22024103R00066